Powercarving

BIRDS, FISH AND PENGUINS

using beautiful hardwoods

Text written with
and photography by
Jeffrey B. Snyder

Schiffer Publishing Ltd
77 Lower Valley Road, Atglen, PA 19310

Gene Larson

Dedication

To Barry and Judy. They made this book happen.

Printed in the United States of America.
ISBN: 0-88740-565-7

We are interested in hearing from authors with book ideas
on related topics.

Published by Schiffer Publishing Ltd.
77 Lower Valley Road
Atglen, PA 19310
Please write for a free catalog.
This book may be purchased from the publisher.
Please include $2.95 postage.
Try your bookstore first.

Contents

Introduction

Whether you enjoy woodcarving animals or creating impressive works of art ... or both, this book is for you. Armed with the information presented here, a band saw, a rotary power tool and a few basic cutting burrs, even the inexperienced carver may turn a block of wood into an amazing representation of one of nature's creatures.

Anyone reading this book can create a wood sculpture. Gene has adapted and simplified many of the methods involved, and readers will be able to use them from page one on. Beginners and "old pro's" alike will quickly grasp -- and be able to use -- the surprisingly simple techniques. Detailed photos (in full color) make each step clear and understandable.

In this, his first book, Gene Larson also explains how *simplicity of form* can be used to convey the full reality of a subject. Just as another artist might create an amazing likeness with only a few lines on paper. Gene sketches in wood, with relatively few lines.

In any kind of art, the viewer sees what the artist *wants* him or her to see: sees detail that isn't really there. Woodcarving is as much an art as sculpture in marble.

Tools

For the projects below, a band saw with a coarse toothed (6/8 tooth per inch or TPI) blade and a rotary cutting tool is needed. The coarse toothed band saw blade will clog less than other blades. Concerning the choice of a rotary tool, I prefer one with 1/4 inch shank capability but if you do not have 1/4 inch capability, 1/8 inch works also. The bit I use the most has a yellow titanium coating on a good burr. The titanium coating will add smoother cutting and a longer life to the burr. Caution: when using these tools, give them your full attention. The cutting burrs do grab the wood; they are aggressive cutters. If you let your attention wander and don't maintain complete control, these burrs can take the skin off your hand in a moment.

For smoothing a piece, I like to use a drum sander on my rotary tool and Swiss Gold sand paper. Swiss Gold is cloth backed, it is flexible and can be wrapped around the drum sander tightly and will last longer than paper backed sandpaper. A Kutzall sleeve on a rubber mandril can also be used to help shape the piece.

The woods used for these projects are, birds-eye maple for the bird, cherry for the fish and butternut for the penguin. If you are new to this equipment and/or to woodcarving, *experiment*. Take pieces of junk wood and carve two or three figures first in each project before moving on to your good wood. I like to use Tung oil as my finish.

Carving the Bird

Top View - Cut This First

The bird as it will look when you are done with this beautiful wood stock.

Center Line

Top View is the Same for All Birds

Side View

Use 2 5/8" Wood for this Peaked Bird

Other Shapes or Make Your Own

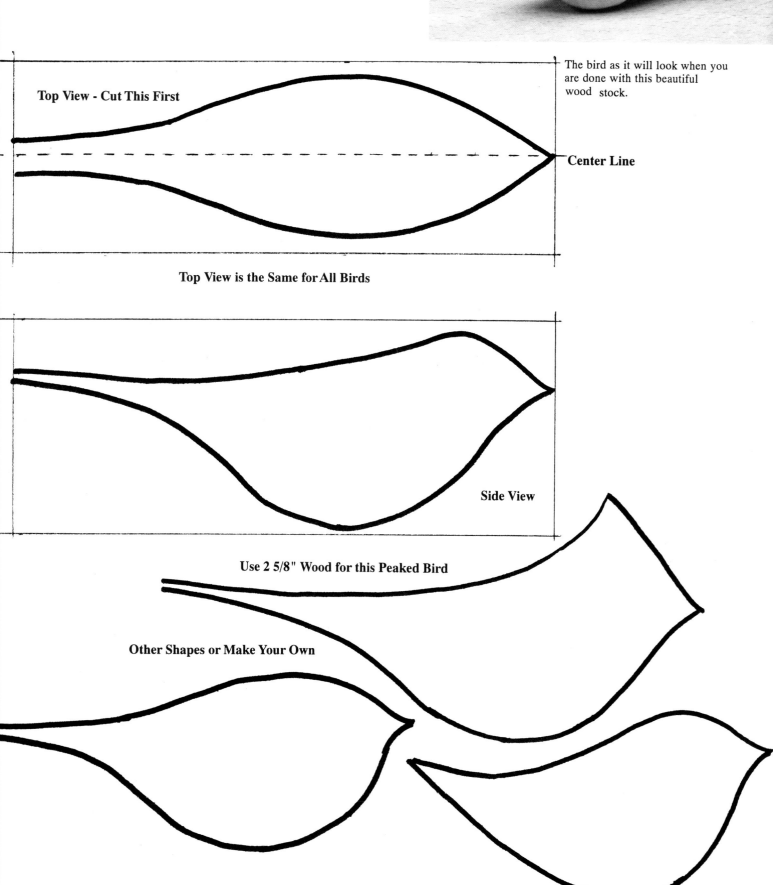

We will be using birds-eye maple for this project because of its beauty. The block of wood used will be approximately 5 3/4" long, 2 1/4" high, and 1 3/4 to 2" thick.

I recommend that you cut the top view first, following the outline. By cutting the top view first, you will have an easier time cutting the side view because you will only have two pieces to replace to provide a stable base for the side view work.

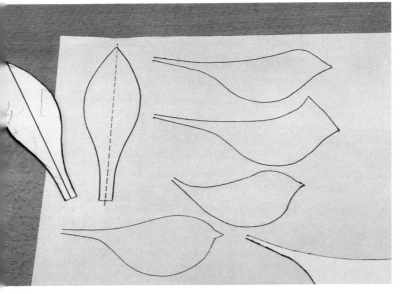

To transfer a pattern to the wood, make a cardboard cut-out of the pattern.

Transfer the pattern you have chosen to the block of wood with a pencil.

Both pieces removed.

Replace the two pieces cut away. In order to keep the loose pieces from slipping it is not a bad idea to use tape with two sticky sides, or a loop of masking tape, which will help keep the wood together while cutting out the side profiles.

Here is the roughed-out bird with the block cut away.

Cut the side profiles.

Now it is time to round the corners with your band saw, following the lines drawn on the rough-cut bird. To do this reset your saw table to 20 degrees. This allows for safer sawing, the work remains flat on the table while the angled cut is accomplished. Four cuts will be made.

Make sure you have enough clearance beneath the blade guard for the head to pass through. The head is the highest point. Do a dry run before cutting rather than attempting this while the blade is running.

Experiment at this point: use junk wood first to carve two or three birds before moving on to your good wood. Making the corner cuts I have shown deeper or shallower changes the character of your bird considerably. Once you have done this with your scrap wood birds, move on to the "good wood" bird using the cuts you preferred.

Both side views cut away.

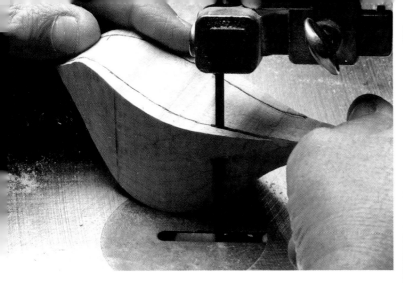

Now, round the top.

The head clears the blade guard easily while rounding the bird.

The rounded bird. You are now done with the band saw.

Rounding the bottom edge of the bird.

Don't throw out the scraps of your pretty wood at this stage. You may wish to use some of the pieces later as imaginative bases or ornaments.

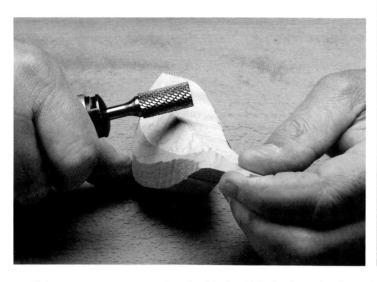

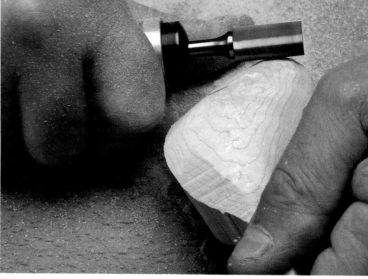

Using your rotary powered tool with the 1/4" shank cutting burr, continue shaping.

Round from the back to the front.

The regular 1/4" cutting burr shown here may produce unwanted straight lines in your work as you can see. If you have this trouble, you may want to use a round-nosed burr. It will keep you from cutting those unwanted lines.

See how smooth the work is with the cutting burr. This reduces the amount of sanding needed later.

I like to leave the bird's belly wider than it's top. This gives more stability for the rocking or "personality" of the bird. We round the bottom to get the bird to rock as well. Try to cut with the grain rather than into the grain, allowing a smoother cut while avoiding potential catching of the burr in the grain. Cutting across the grain is fine also and sharp tools will leave a nice smooth edge.

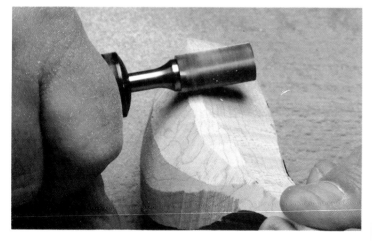

Rounding down one side.

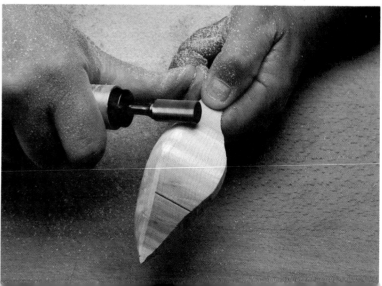

Cutting with the grain. In this case the grain runs from the birds belly in the direction of the beak. The grain of each wood may react differently from the next piece, it is necessary to experiment.

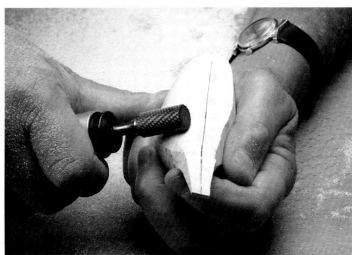

Rounding down using the center line as a guide.

Rounding down the belly, neck and beak.

At this point start looking at the bird from this angle to keep both sides even. Draw a center line to help check the balance.

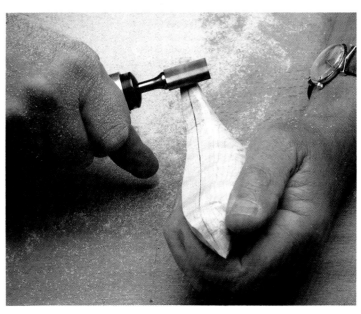

Reverse directions to smooth down the tail of the bird, following the grain to the back.

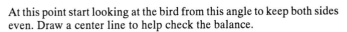

At this point I have turned the bird over with the tail facing me. I'm going to be tapering the wood from the center of the tail to approximately the line shown on the edge of the tail. This is forming the juncture of the body and the tail. Thin deeper in the direction of the arrows towards the indicated line. If you feel it is necessary then draw the line to be your guide.

Thinning one side of the tail. You can make the tail quite thin with most hardwoods. However it is probably a good idea to do your final thinning with sandpaper rather than a cutting burr.

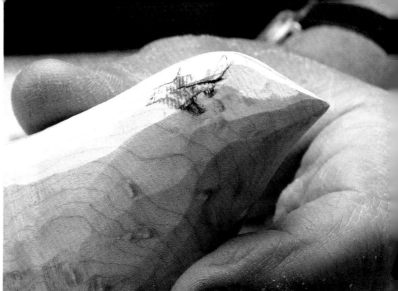

Round down the other side, beginning at the center line and working out.

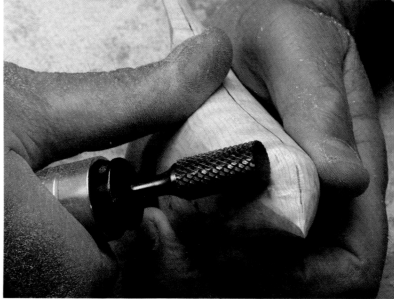

Round down the marked high spot.

If you can do it by eye, holding the bird up while you round, so much the better. If you take off too much, don't shoot yourself. Just take some more off the other side to match. This is your bird..

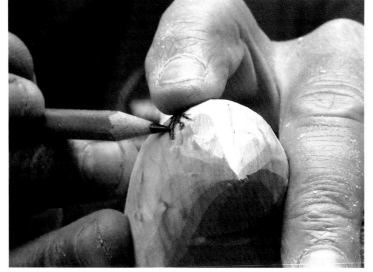

As you round down, look for high spots. Put your finger on the problem area and mark it with a pencil.

I did not want to chance the cutting burr catching here because I was going into the grain. I turned the angle and cut at a right angle to the grain, minimizing the possibility of catching around the peak at the edge of the belly.

The cutting burr will also remove the vertical lines left by the band saw more quickly than sandpaper.

Your bird should be looking like this now. It's time to move on to the sanding.

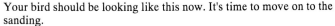

We are using a sanding drum and Swiss Gold sand paper. Either 100 or 120 grit is a good starting grit for the sand paper. We will switch to 220 grit when nearly finished. 320 grit is my final paper. Later we will take the 220 grit paper in hand directly to manually sand the bird, removing all the remaining little scratches.

Sand down the bird, moving with the grain. If you sand at right angles you will get scratches that are much harder to remove.

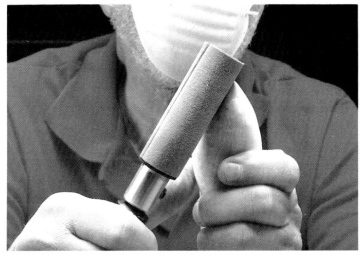

The smooth cylinder of the sanding drum makes a good straight edge guide. Slowly sand alongside the head and beak area, using the drum's side to keep this area straight as well as smooth. Flip the bird over and sand the corresponding side straight.

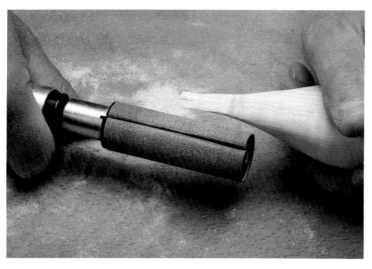

The same technique may also be used along the tail.

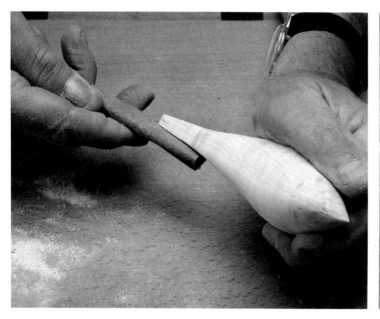

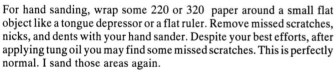

For hand sanding, wrap some 220 or 320 paper around a small flat object like a tongue depressor or a flat ruler. Remove missed scratches, nicks, and dents with your hand sander. Despite your best efforts, after applying tung oil you may find some missed scratches. This is perfectly normal. I sand those areas again.

Use the hand sanding to round the ends of the tail.

Your sanded bird should look like this.

Now it is time to apply the tung oil. I use a few different finishes. Tung oil goes on easily. I like to use both high and semi-gloss. Depending on your wood, it may take as many as five coats to give you the desired finish. Using 0000 grade steel wool between each coat is a good idea if you want a really smooth finish. Rags or paper towels work for applying the tung oil. Follow application directions on the container. Wait for each coat to dry before applying the next coat.

A clear urethane spray also makes a good, fast drying finish but be sure to use it in a well ventilated area. Apply with very light coats. Once again, high or low gloss is available depending on your taste.

Here is our bird with tung oil applied to the back half.

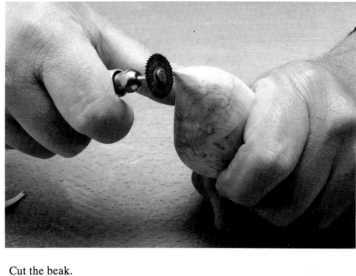

Cut the beak.

The first full coat of tung oil has been applied.

If desired, a thin slit can be cut into the beak using your rotary tool with a small saw blade on a 1/8" shank. Caution: do not attempt this operation if there are any distractions near you. Besides being dangerous, cutting a beak at the wrong angle will make your bird look like it has been out drinking all night. Practice your cut on a scrap or an early practice bird before you make the final cut. You will only have one shot at this one.

The cut is made.

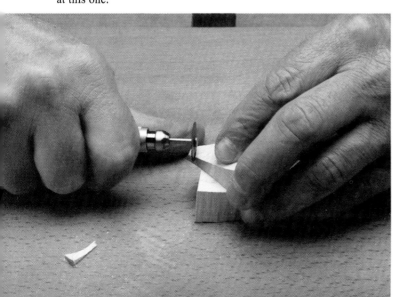

Your bird can now hold a business card or other thin paper.

Remember the scrap wood you didn't throw away? My bird fits well in this piece.

Variations on the basic bird theme.

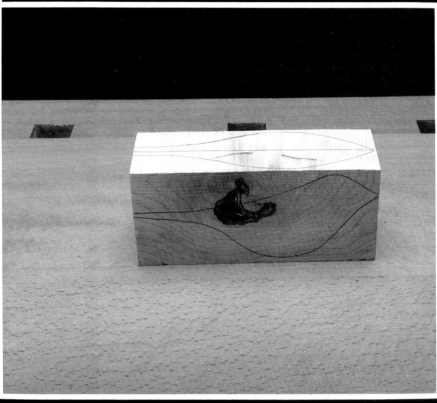

Scraps may also become unique stands or bird-shaped ornaments for windows and trees.

Go ahead, use a piece with an unusual knot or blemish. The end results may be both surprising and beautiful. What have you got to lose?

Carving the Fish

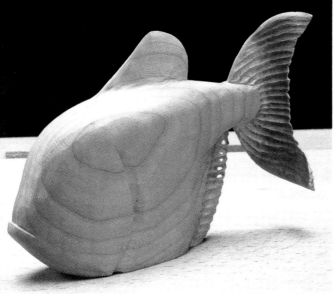

Here is the fish we will carve.

There is more than one way to transfer a pattern from paper to wood stock. Trace or photocopy the pattern for the fish out of the book.

Flip the pattern over and rub over the underside with a lead pencil.

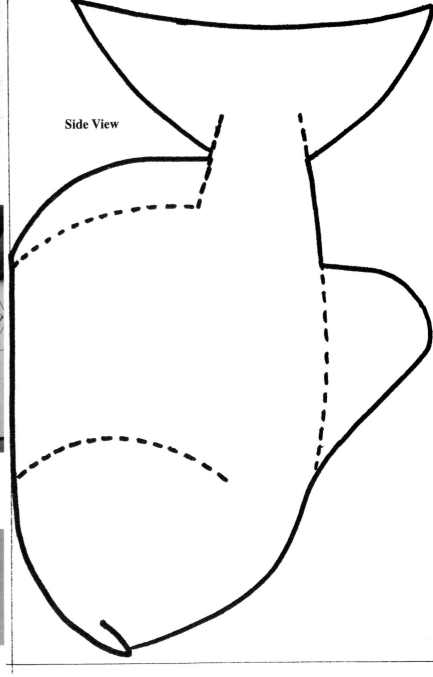

Side View

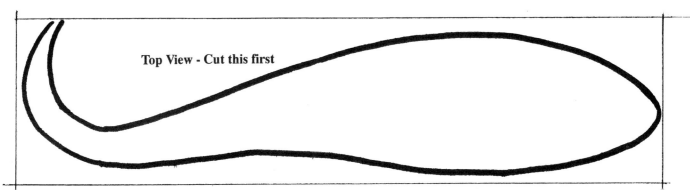

Top View - Cut this first

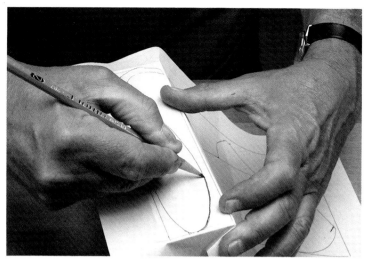

Now place the pattern over a 7" X 4 3/4" X 1 13/16" to 2" block of cherry or other wood. Place graphite to wood and trace over the pattern lines directly with your pencil. A piece of carbon paper will work just as well, eliminating the need for the graphite.

The pattern is transferred to the wood. Retrace it with a pen or marker to make a bold pattern that is easy to follow. If you want a more permanent pattern to use on more than one fish, paste the paper pattern to cardboard and cut the pattern out as a template. For a very fast, one use only method, paste the paper pattern directly on the wood block.

The pattern transferred to the wood.

Cut out the top profile.

Replace the two pieces to cut the side profiles. They will hold the piece square to the bandsaw table and give you a smooth working surface. Cut out the side profile with the band saw.

Do not attempt to cut the excess wood stock away from between the fins. This area is too tight; the right angle turn can't be made with the band saw. Just cut straight across.

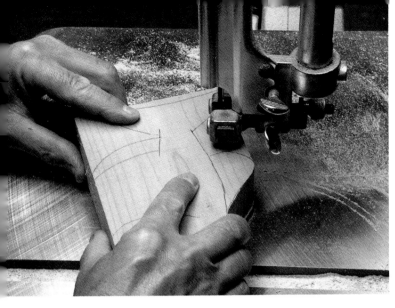

To get into these areas, beginning half way between the dorsal fin and the tail, cut a straight line down to the point where the tail joins the body.

Now cut back along this fin in a straight line.

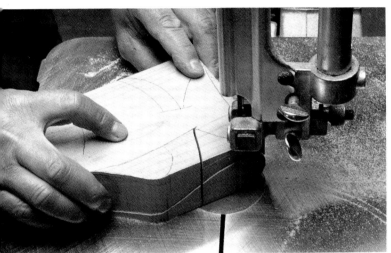

Reverse course and cut a straight line to the point where the dorsal fin connects with the body.

Continue to cut away sections until the material between the fins is gone.

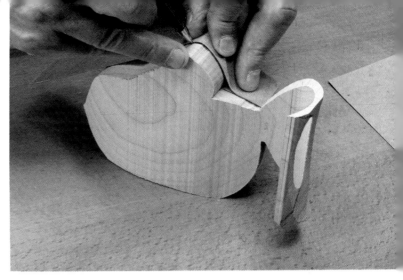

Mark the trailing edges of the tail fin with guide lines. Draw a center line on the top and bottom as well. Remove excess material with either a coping saw or the cutting burr's straight edge. If the trailing edges are to be real thin, support them with your fingers when you cut.

Cut away the extra stock from between the lower fins and around the lower jaw as well.

Cut a flexible cardboard straight edge, mold it along the center line of your fish and mark in the center line around the top and bottom of the fish in sections until the center line is complete. This will guide the future shaping of your fish.

Carve the curving edge of the tail with a rotary tool and a cutting burr. I ended up with an unexpected hole. But that is not a real problem, you will see.

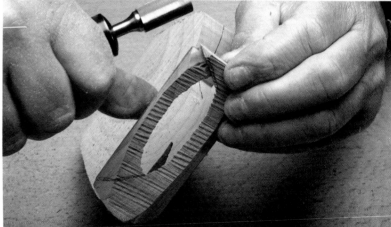

Carefully and slowly work away the excess material, supporting your edges and keeping the cutting burr from getting trapped in the center hole.

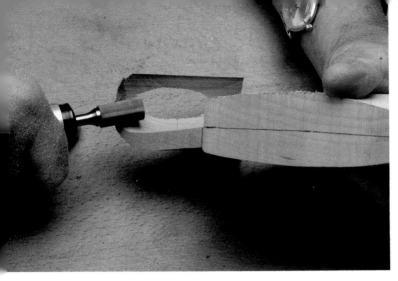

While you have the extra support, shape the delicate trailing edges of the tail.

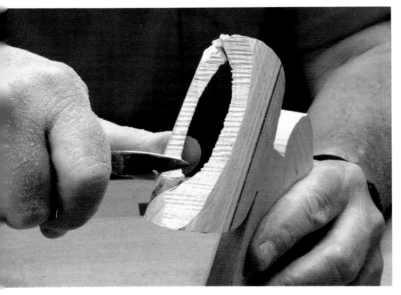

The final removal of the excess material may be accomplished with a carving knife once the cutting burr has created a deep groove to follow.

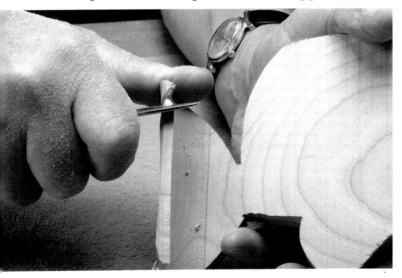

Working in from the delicate outer edge puts the force of each cut into the thicker central area, reducing pressure on the trailing edge of the fin.

Redraw the pattern details which were removed when the extra stock was cut away on the bandsaw. You will need these guides for shaping with the cutting burr. Remember, you do not have to make these guides exact. This is your fish, if you want the gills in a different shape go ahead and make them so.

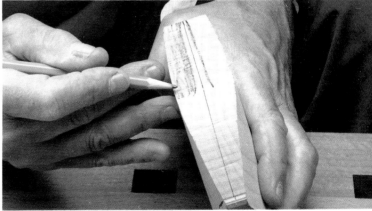

Now eyeball in the thickness of the dorsal fin. Remove excess stock, making the fin roughly 1/4" thick at the juncture with the body and tapering it to 1/8" at the top of the dorsal fin. This will leave plenty of stock for later reduction to a nice thin fin.

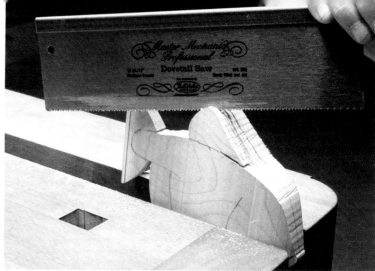

One method of removing excess wood from the dorsal fin area is to make a saw cut from the top of the fin down to the body of the fish. The smaller the saw the easier it will be to control the cut. I like to use a miter saw which has a reinforced back for added rigidity. A coping saw works well also.

Once the first cut down to the top of the body is made, cut in along the top of the body. Avoid cutting too deeply and shearing off the dorsal fin in the process.

Be aware of the position of your fish tail. Don't cut it with the miter saw.

You will meet the vertical cut at the front but not at the back of the dorsal fin.

If you can't reach the body of the fish in the back because of the tail, just make two cuts for each side on an angle where you will be missing the tail area.

Pivot the saw to make the cut join the back vertical cut on the dorsal fin. Don't worry about making it neat. Whatever excess remains will be removed anyway.

Cut away as much as you can without cutting into the body of the fish.

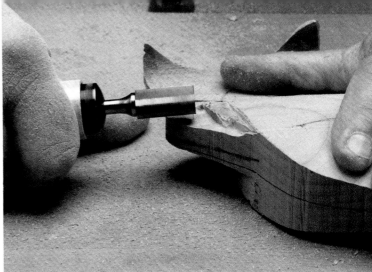

Keep removing material a little at a time until you reach the guide lines.

The excess wood is removed from one half of the fin.

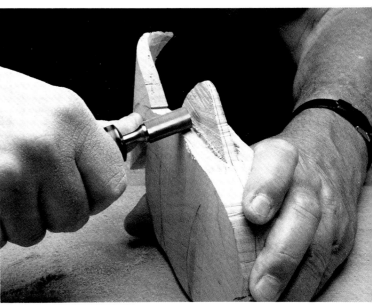

Now, to take off the remaining excess at the juncture of the dorsal fin and the fish body, use the cutting burr.

If you don't have a vice to hold the fish or a saw to remove the excess wood from the dorsal fin, you can always use your trusty rotary tool. Using the flat edge of the cutter, which works as a wonderful burr for creating sharp straight lines, use it for defining the body and dorsal fin. The juncture between fin and body is a good place to start. If you don't have a 1/4" shank tool, by all means use your 1/8" cutting burr which will do the same job but which will take longer.

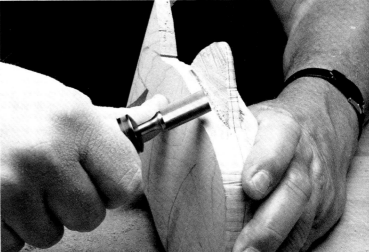

You may round down the body a little now as well. Do not come too close to the juncture of the dorsal fin and body, you don't want to create an undercut.

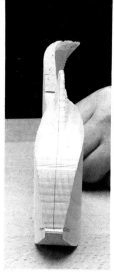

The fin should look like this now.

Use the center line as your guide in thinning the dorsal fin. Come right up to it at the top of the fin.

Here is a finished dorsal on a zebra wood fish which will give you a better idea of what you are trying to accomplish.

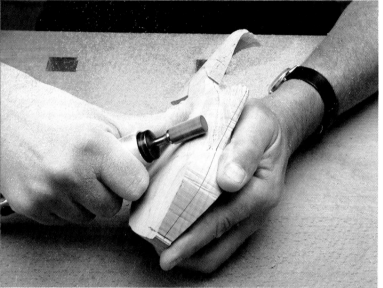

I like to work on roughing out the body next rather than the tail because the tail will be the thinnest and most vulnerable to breakage, so let's leave that for later.

Round down to the mouth. You may have a fish with a broad forehead or a fish with a narrower one depending on how much material you decide to remove.

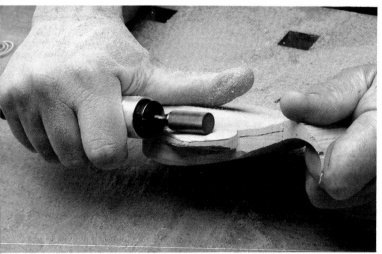

Round down the dorsal fin as well, thinning it down very narrow at the top to about 1/8" thick or less at the base. Make this fin as thin as you feel comfortable making it.

Begin defining the base of the tail area. Using the edge of the cutting burr, follow the pencil mark, starting to define the details as penciled in.

Now I have rounded down the area from the mouth back along the top to the tail and the dorsal fin as well as outlining the base of the tail.

To round down the base of the dorsal fin, move the cutting burr gently backward along the juncture of the fin and the body.

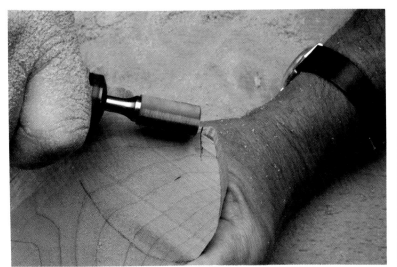

Using a series of short strokes (don't try to do this all in one cut) cut in the outline of the mouth from above. Leave a jutting lower lip, a fish with an attitude.

Before you begin to define the details of the gills and the juncture of the tail, you will want to make sure that the patterns you transferred back onto the wood earlier are even. To accomplish this place your finger along the upper edge of the gill ...

... and while looking from the front of the fish you can now eyeball a pencil mark into the same location on the other side of the body top to bottom.

To locate the same point from front to back repeat this procedure while looking from above.

Another way to keep the pattern lines even is to photocopy this little ruler or redraw your own. If you redraw your own ruler, make sure your markings are all equally spaced to retain accuracy. Lay the ruler along the center line and count down the number of marks to the top edge of the gill in this case.

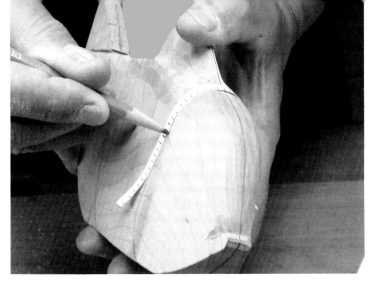

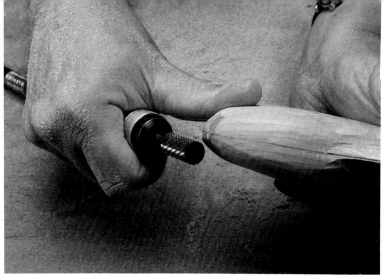

Count down the same number of marks on the other side of the fish and make your mark for the top edge of the gill on the other side. This method will work well to line up any two points on both sides of your carving evenly.

Round off the sharp corners of the mouth.

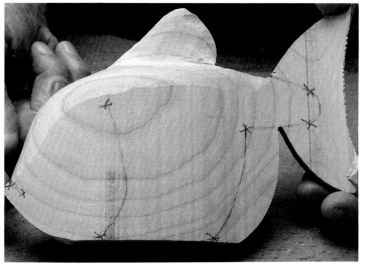

Repeat this procedure for each of the points marked with an X on this fish. This way you won't have a lopsided fish.

At this point, if you are going to mount your fish as part of a larger sculpture, round off the entire bottom area. If you intend to leave it free standing, leave the bottom flat.

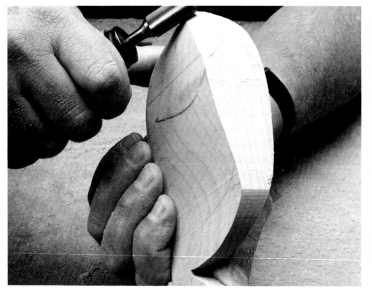

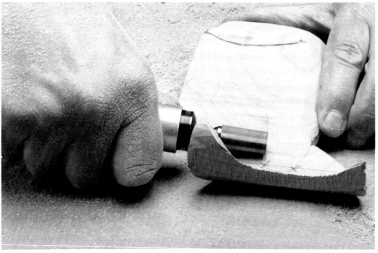

Now begin to round off the lower jaw of the fish.

Now begin rounding out the tail, gills and other features using the straight edge of the cutting burr. Keep the cuts to approximately 1/16" deep to give good definition.

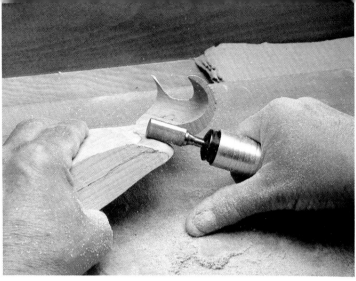

Each cut along the juncture of the tail has two sides, creating a V shaped definition line. The gills and lower back fin do not.

Continue to reduce the stock and create the curve of the lower fin.

Begin removing stock from the lower back fin, curving the back fin in the opposite direction to the curve of the tail fin, accentuating a sense of motion between the two fins. To do this aim for the far corner along the opposite edge of the fin.

To reduce tight areas on the lower back fin near the tail, use a 1/8" shank Rotary tool with a 1/4" ball cutter. It gives you freer access and greater control to reduce gradually in tight spots.

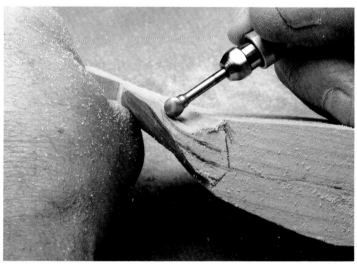

Drawing a center line and guide lines on the base of the fish and checking it frequently as you remove stock will make reducing the lower back fin easier. Cut down until you have 1/8" worth of material on each side of the center line.

Use the 1/4" ball cutter to remove stock from the inside of the curve of the lower back fin where things get tight.

If you should make a mistake and go through the wood when creating a scallop, go ahead and incorporate the mistake into the piece. I repeated the pattern here to good effect.

As you scoop out the interior of the fin you can start placing the swirls or scallops in the fin itself.

You will find that getting into the juncture between the body and lower back fin is difficult unless you start cutting down the thickness of the tail also. That's fine. Do it.

Round down the area where the lower back fin meets the body of the fish so there is no ledge but a gradual sloping into the body. The ball cutter does this well.

During this operation I use my fingers as a rough caliper, feeling the thickness I can not see.

Round in the same way along the shaft of the tail.

Here you see the stock has been reduced to the center line.

Begin to thin the tail while you are here. The ball cutter will define the edge of the tail around your guide lines well.

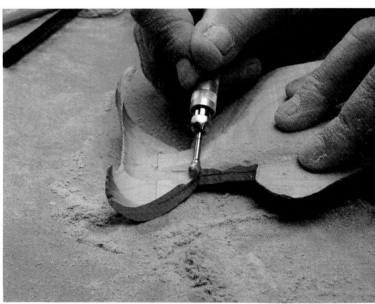

Taper the upper inside edge to the center line as well.

Work outward from the center of the tail toward the lower edge. Thin from the inside of the curve out to the bottom center line to give a sense of motion along the lower edge. Let the cutter do the work, don't push down hard.

Repeat the process on the outside of the tail. Outline first.

Taper down to the center line along the outer edges of the tail.

Be very careful down here at the tip of the tail. Either be gentle or keep your glue handy.

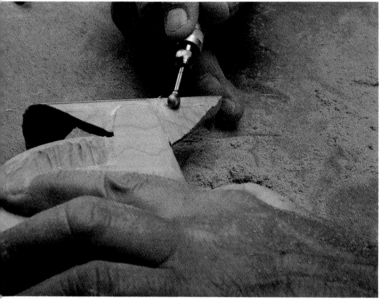

Continue thinning down the body of the tail, check regularly with your fingers to make sure you are leaving enough material so as not to cut through the center of the tail. If you are bashful about removing stock from the center of the tail, be sure the outer edges come to a nice sharp edge and this will create an illusion of thinness.

The roughed out fish should look like this.

We have one flat edge at the back of the tail where a hole was created by the bandsaw. To continue the flowing line of the tail, soften that hard edge by reducing it with the ball cutter.

Smooth down around the base of the dorsal fin. Use a light touch here.

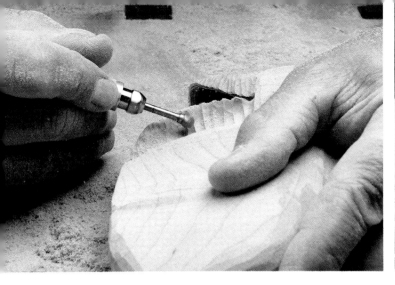

Now begin to lay in the grooves along the lower fin and the tail, laying each groove side-by-side, creating little peaks between them. Take the grooves all the way to the edge of the fin. Remember to keep checking the thickness.

Here is the other side of the bottom fin and the tail with the scalloping complete.

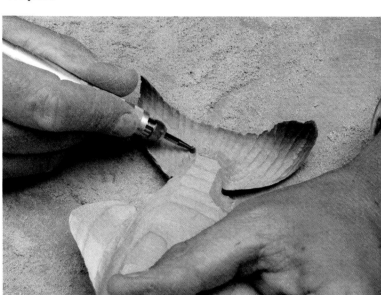

To create the scallops in the tail, begin in the center and work out, always checking your thickness, and bringing the scallops out to the very edge of the tail. Also I fan the scallops out at a gradually increasing angle to follow the shape of the tail .

Switch to a 1/8" cutting ball from the 1/4" ball previously used. Go in and give a little added detail to the tail and start to clean up small areas elsewhere that are still rough. Here we are adding definition and depth to the base of the tail.

Here are the scalloped lines on both the tail and the lower back fin complete on one half of the carving. Bringing the scallops all the way to the edge of the fin gives it a nice, slightly ragged look.

Here I am adding definition to the base of the lower back fin.

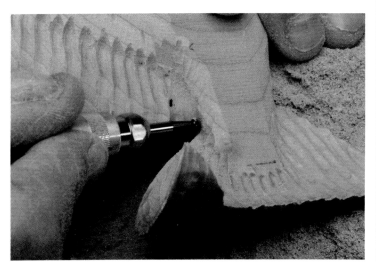

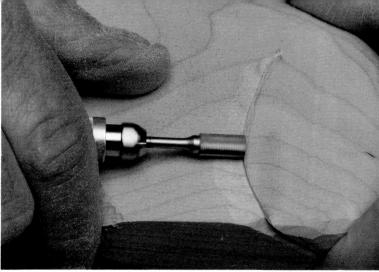

The 1/8" cutting ball also helps round in small areas like this one between the tail and the lower back fin.

The 1/4" cutting burr adds definition and smooths the rough cuts around the gill.

A knife will also get into those small areas.

The 1/4" cutting burr also works well for cleaning up around the other detailed areas of the fish.

At this point you also want to define the gills along the underside of the fish.

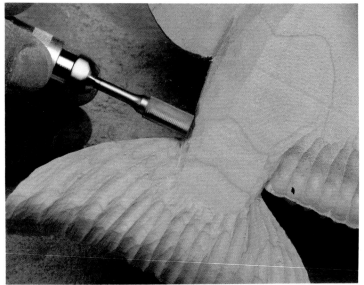

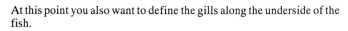

A small 1/8" shank with a 1/4" cutting burr is used to add fine line definition in the tail, the fin, the gill and the mouth areas.

Using a sanding drum with Swiss Gold sand paper (starting with 120 grit and working your way up to 220 then 320) work on the side of the fish first, sanding with the grain as much as possible. The side is an open area that will give you the feel of the sander before you get into the details. Use good light and take your time. You can ruin all your good work with a poor sanding job.

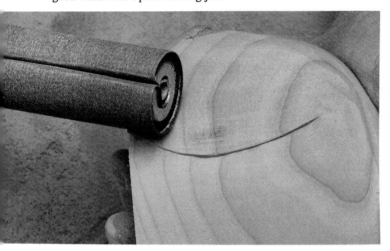

Make sure to sand away any band saw marks.

Run your sander along the length of the tail to flatten the rough edges out, leaving a smooth but flattened edge. Hand sanding will accomplish the same task if you are bashful about using the power sanding drum.

You will have rough edges like this along the edge of the tail.

The new smooth but flattened tail edge.

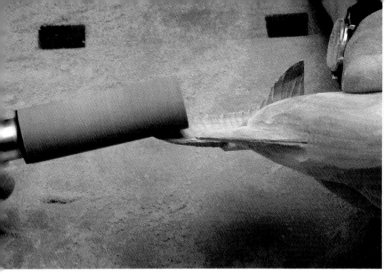

Next use the sander at an angle to reestablish a nice sharp edge to the tail.

Work the sander over the fish to round, smooth and add final shaping. Here I am working around the dorsal fin, evening out each side of the body and sharpening the leading edge of the fin. Make sure to hold the fish up to good light at many different angles to assure you remove all the scratches and marks left by the sander. Never leave the sander in one spot or it will dig in.

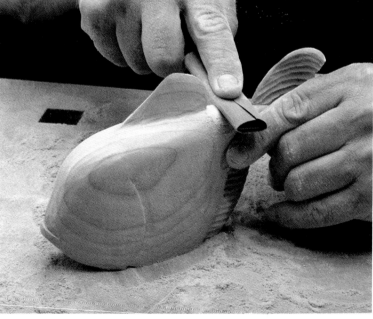

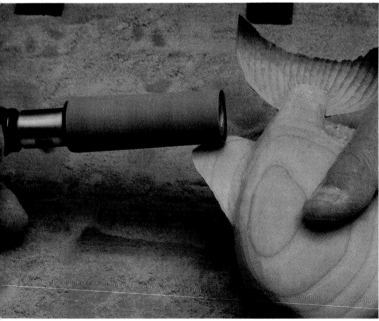

Use the sander to smooth and sharpen the edges of the dorsal fin as well. But be careful here not to break the fin or to reshape it if you do.

Use any small, flat piece of wood (like a tongue depressor) wrapped in sand paper to get into places the drum sander can't handle.

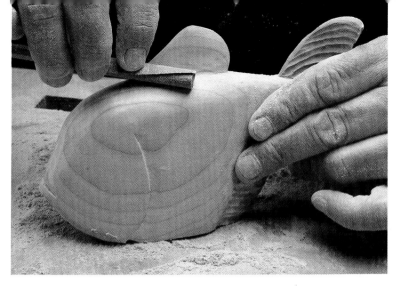

A dowel rod or a pencil will also get you into hard to reach places with your sand paper.

Working with the small 1/8" ball cutter I added a hole to each scallop in the fin, turning a mistake into a design.

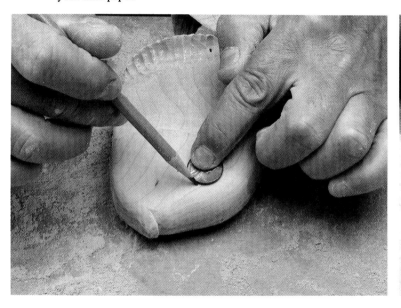

If you want eyes, a penny will give you the circle and the measuring technique we discussed earlier will help you place them. Use the small 1/4" cutter to gently outline the eyes you desire. Go back with the small ball to round them out. Then sand them.

How's that? Transformed from a single mistake hole into an artistic detail!

Ah ha! I thought I was done but my eagle-eyed editor spotted this hole where the wood became too thin and he challenged me to make it work or make a new fish for this book. Being lazy, I took the challenge! Here's what I did.

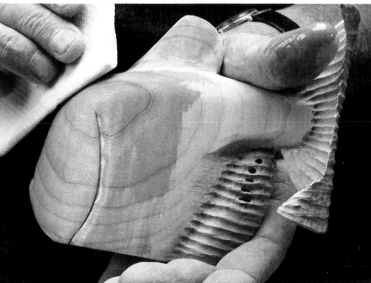

Finally apply your finish. In this case I'm using tung oil.

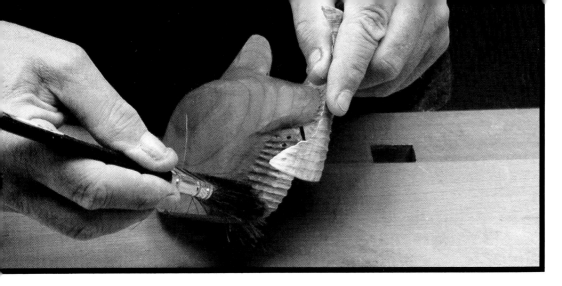

An inexpensive bristle brush is good for applying tung oil to hard-to-reach places.

The oil is applied.

Mount those fish if you wish to create a finished scene.

Carving the Penguin

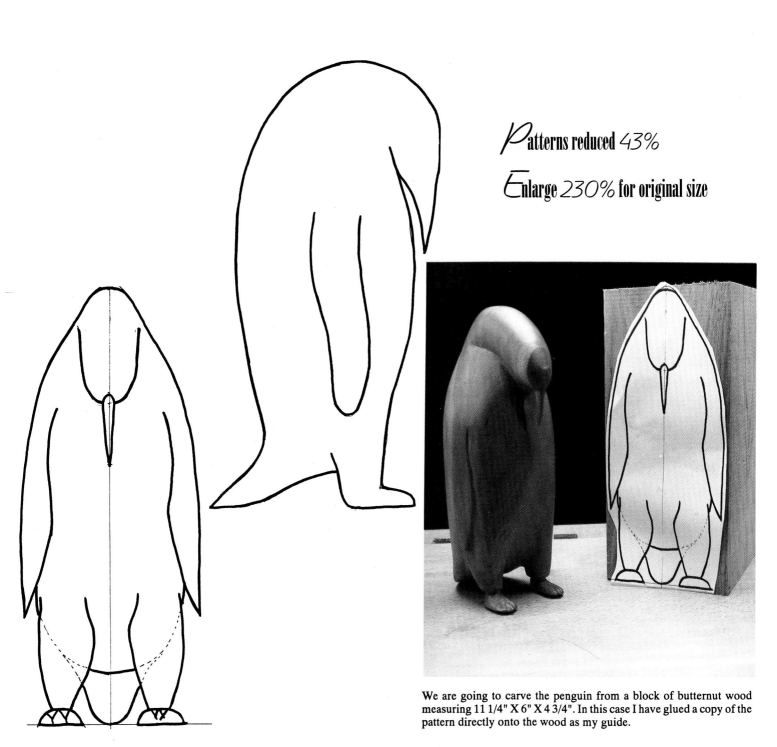

Patterns reduced 43%

Enlarge 230% for original size

We are going to carve the penguin from a block of butternut wood measuring 11 1/4" X 6" X 4 3/4". In this case I have glued a copy of the pattern directly onto the wood as my guide.

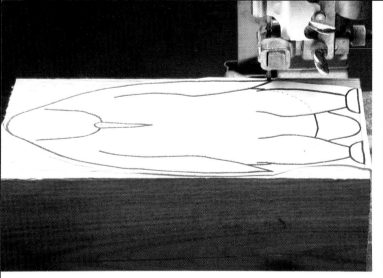

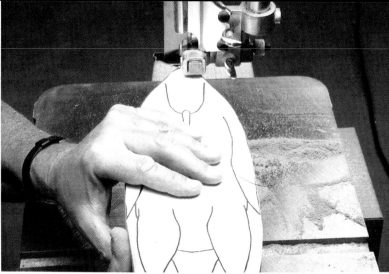

The blade guard has been raised here to show the cutting process more clearly. In reality, it should be as close to the work as possible to avoid bending the blade or cutting yourself. Once your guard is properly adjusted, first cut out one side of the front pattern. Cutting the sides first will allow you to use the smooth sides as supports later just as with the bird and the fish. Don't try to cut out the details of the wings at this time.

Round off the top of the head.
To remove material between the wings:

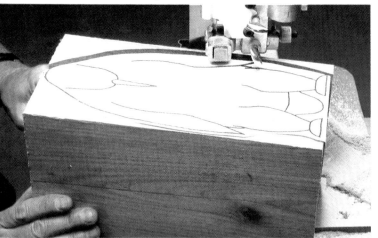

One side is cut.

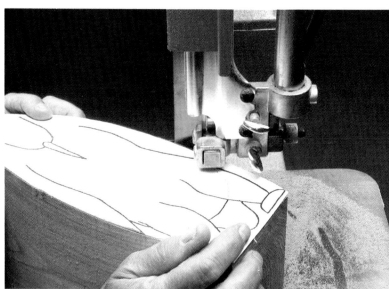

Cut in along the lower edge of the wing.

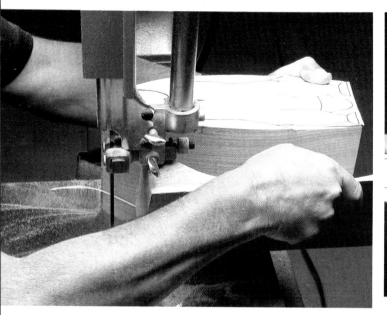

The second side is cut.

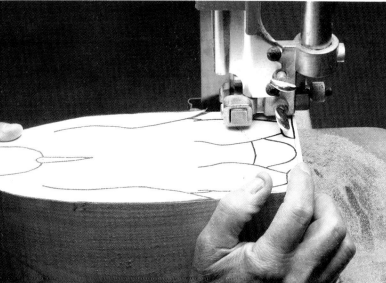

Cut a straight line from the edge of the foot up to the cut inner end of the wing and remove the excess wood.

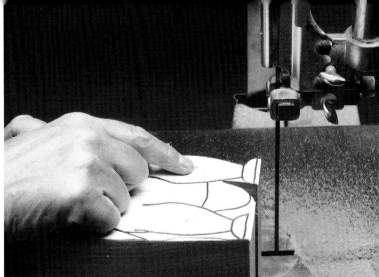

Next cut back into the corner of the foot to remove the extra stock from above the foot.

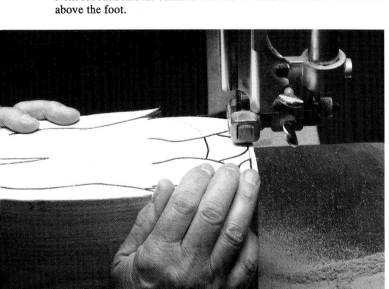

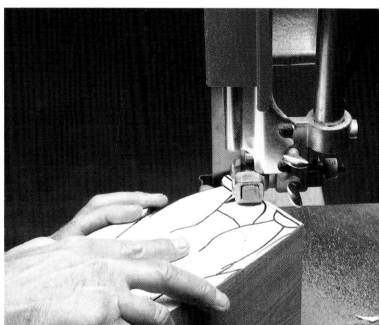

To remove the stock from between the legs and tail, first cut a line from the foot to the tail edge to the inner point where the leg meets the body.

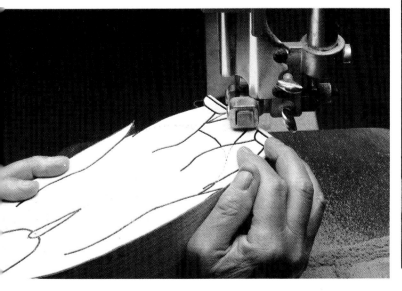

Cut another line along the tail pattern up to the same corner and remove the stock.

Cut the remaining stock loose in small bits. Cut a series of straight lines to the leg first and then cut up from the foot up the leg to chew away the rest. Repeat this procedure for the other wing and foot.

The first cut comes loose.

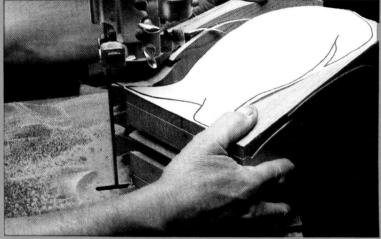

Now you have the front profile.

The second cut comes loose.

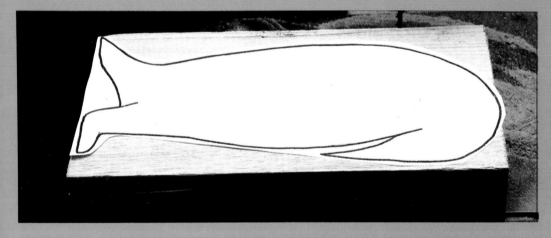

Use masking tape to reattach the large cut side panels. Fasten the side profile to one of the reattached side panels.

Cut around the side profile of the penguin. Do not try to get into the inner areas between the beak and belly, between the belly and feet or between the feet and tail yet.

Remove the material from the beak and belly area following both guide lines carefully. Just be sure to back the saw out slowly after each cut. Follow the same procedures as before for removing excess material around the feet and tail.

The cut out figure of the penguin.

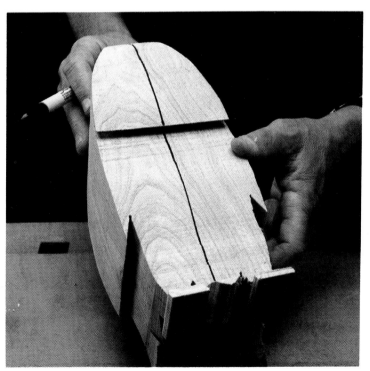

Draw in your center line.

Place your pattern back on the penguin. Another way to do this is to inscribe the pattern into the wood with a knife.

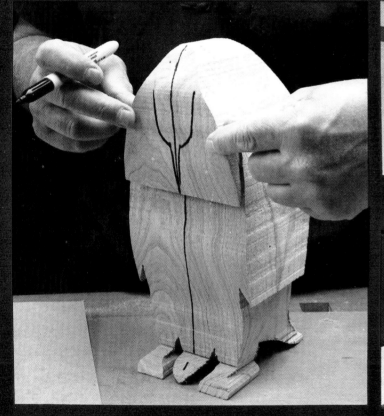

Now it is time to remove the excess from the shoulder areas I am pointing to.

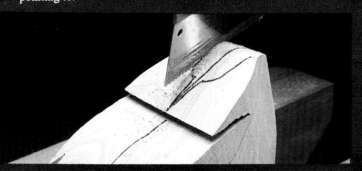

Use a vise and a miter saw to remove the excess material. Tilting the saw outward away from the head, saw along the line of the head.

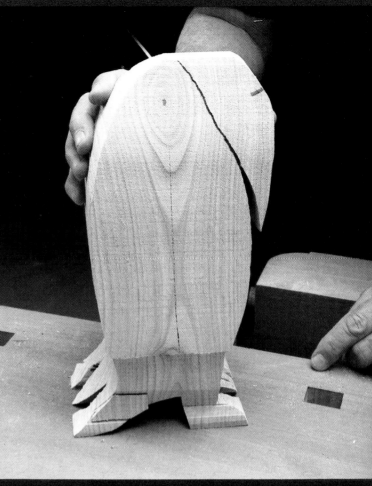

I have drawn a continuation of the beak line and that is what I will saw down to.

Cutting along the extended beak line will help move the process along.

The first cut comes away. Repeat these steps on the other side.

Now we will remove the excess material from between the front legs, the material in the back becomes the tail.

Continue removing the excess. Right now you need not worry about ragged edges as there will be more wood to remove from higher between the legs before we are done.

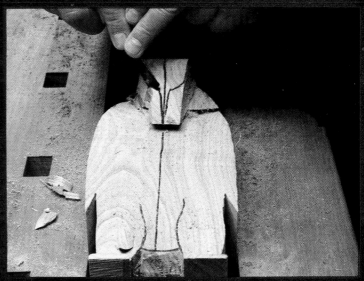

Use the miter saw to remove the excess material. First cut straight down to the juncture of the leg and belly on both sides.

Now remove the excess wood from around the beak. Use the chisel, working at an angle away from the head and beak. Remove the excess, following the contour of the head. Butternut is very workable by hand but if you are using a harder wood, use your power tool with a 1/4 or 1/8 inch flat end cylinder cutting burr.

Using a chisel, start working away the excess wood. If you prefer, you can use your rotary cutter; however, on butternut I enjoy the feel of the chisel on the wood.

This is what the roughed out beak should look like.

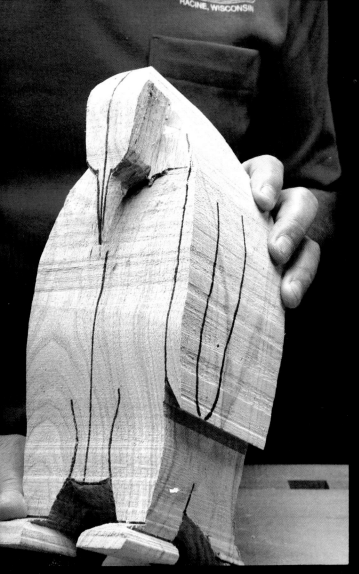

Turn the piece on its side to define the leading edge of the wing.

The leading edge of the wing with the stock removed. Moving on to define the back of the wing.

Draw in the pattern of the wing on your roughed wood penguin.

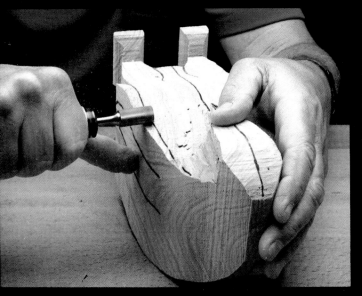

Remove the excess wood following the guidelines, using the 1/4" cutting burr. Remove the stock first from the top down to define the line of the side of the chest.

Now use the edge of the cutting burr to define the back edge of the wing.

Move on to remove wood up to the trailing edge of the wing.

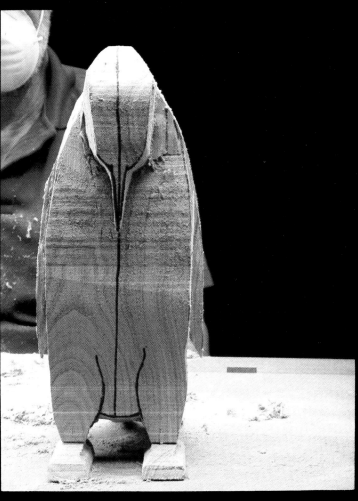

Front and side views of the roughed out wing. See how it tapers into the upper body.

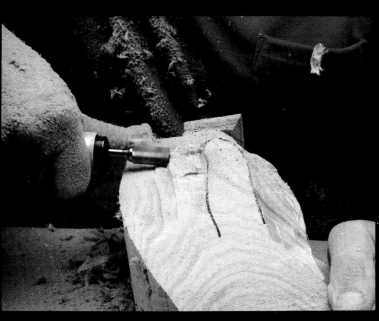

You will remove more stock at the base of the wing where it hangs down away from the penguin and gradually less up to the shoulder area where the wing blends into the body.

Remove the excess stock from around the tail , the area marked in on the photograph.

Begin with a fairly shallow angled cut along the back line of the penguin's leg. No deeper than shown here.

The next cut with the miter saw roughly follows the line of the tail across the back of the extra stock.

When the two cut lines meet you have removed as much of the excess stock as you need to with the miter saw. The extra leg is gone. Notice how this helps to define the back of the leg.

Now we need to remove the excess stock from around the tail and rear leg area.

I like to define the limit of my cut using the edge of my cutting burr along the line on the body. You could also make small saw cuts to remove some of this stock and outline the limits.

Remove the excess stock.

Here is the end result of the rough shaping of the tail area.

Here is how the area should look, following the line marked on the back and the back of the leg while tapering the underbody into a rounded "football" shape. Notice that we have been uncovering knots in the wood. I don't have a problem with them, in fact I feel they add character to the Penguin.

Now that all of the excess stock has been taken away, it is time to start rounding, to start closing in on the final shape.

Start rounding the back working from the outside in to the center line. Don't be afraid to remove a large amount of stock here, square penguins aren't very "penguinesque."

You will first round down a large amount of excess stock from the center line on the back to within roughly 1/2" of the edge of the wing as noted with the marked line.

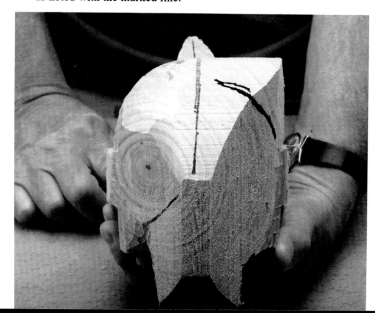

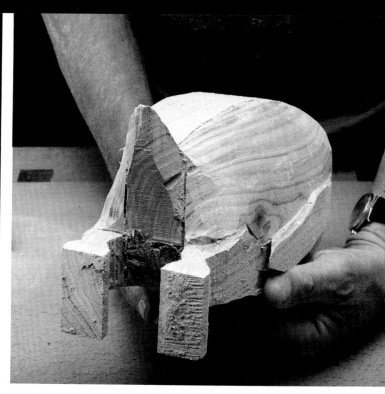

See how the back tapers into the tail

The first rounded side as compared to the unrounded back.

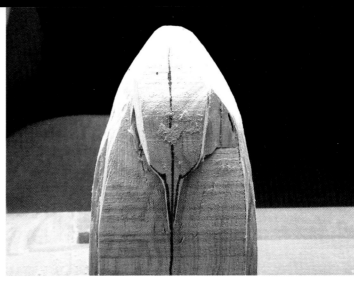

Now it is time to start rounding down the top of the head.

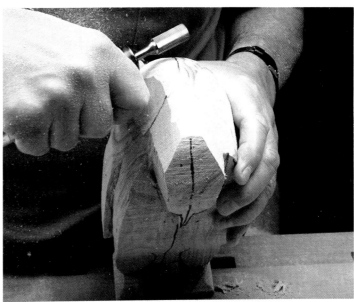

Begin rounding down. Continue until the top looks roughly like a half circle.

Here is the fully rounded back. Make sure to follow earlier instructions to keep both sides even.

Until the top of the head looks like this, that is.

Continue down the head area rounding it out.

Here is how the rounded half of the head compares with the unrounded half.

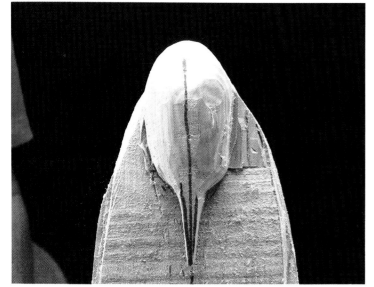

The rounded head.

Now draw in the pattern for the neck from your paper pattern.

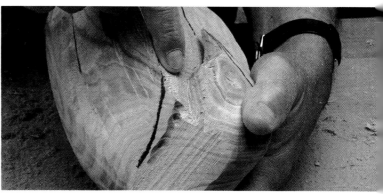

Switch to the ball-nosed cutting burr to define the neck. You are going to be blending from here at the bottom of the head up along the pattern line of the neck.

Follow the line of the neck and begin removing the excess stock.

Continue to remove stock.

The end result of defining half the neck. Now use the techniques we discussed earlier to locate the same neck line along the other half of the penguin and repeat the rounding down procedure.

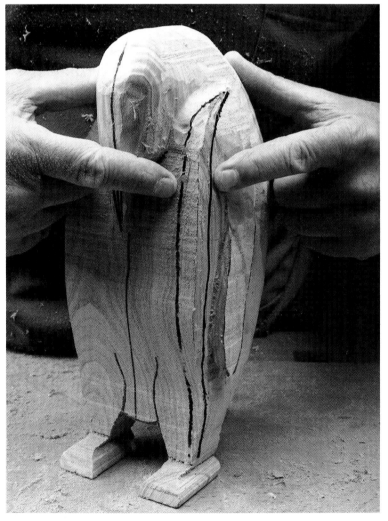

Now we will begin rounding the front of the body, starting with the shoulder. Continue using the ball-nosed cutting burr to round down the excess material between the drawn lines from the shoulder down to the wing. Don't be afraid to remove some wood here.

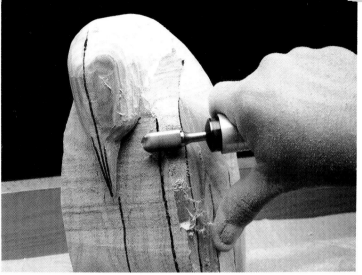

Rounding down the front of the body.

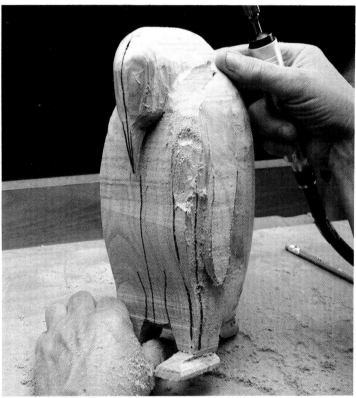

See the area indicated for rounding the front all the way down the leg. See what has been accomplished in the shoulder and upper chest so far.

Rounding out the lower front leg and belly. The butternut I am using peels away quite easily. You may be using wood that only comes off as sawdust.

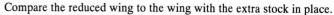

Now half of the front is rounded down. Notice the difference in appearance.

Trim down to the line with the ball-nosed cutting burr.

Compare the reduced wing to the wing with the extra stock in place.

You want to remove excess stock from the wing in order to give it a little shape following the guide line you see here. This is a gentle sweep. How you want this to look is really up to you. Be creative.

Now it is time to round down the beak. First mark the beak pattern from the paper pattern onto the rough beak like this.

Stop when the beak has been rounded down about 1/8" as seen here.

Now we will round down about 1/8" with the ball-nosed cutting burr, as shown here in the line on the side view.

Now continue to gently round the sharp corners of the beak. We will discuss the treatment of the bottom part of the beak a little later.

Working from the center of the beak, round down towards the top line across the beak.

For now the beak should look like this.

Begin shaping the leg area and the underbelly. Remove the excess stock from the underbelly first with the ball-nosed cutting burr.

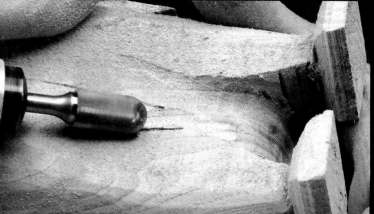

Round the underbelly up to the sides of the leg and create the slope in front where the underbelly begins to slide back under the penguin.

Taper the underbelly back along the line of the tail.

Now round the angular edges around the legs and blend them in with the body where they join.

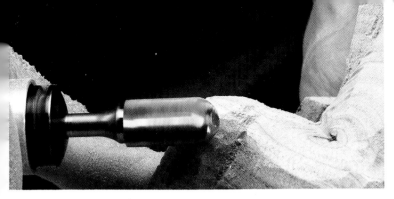

This is a good time to begin rounding the heels on the penguin as well.

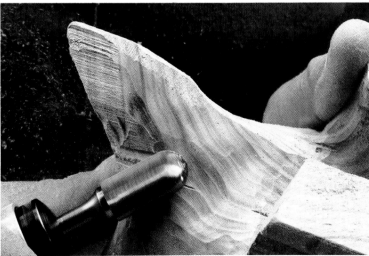

Round the underside of the tail, removing any remaining saw marks in the process. Don't worry about being too neat, sanding will remove the roughness.

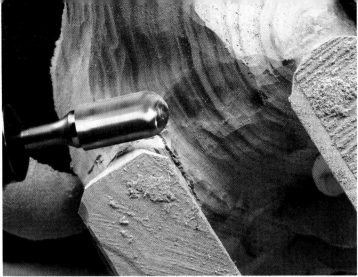

Rounding the back of the other foot.

Now switch to the 1/8" shank cutting burr. It is fun to play with the shape of the foot. Let's cut the feet down more by removing the excess stock from the heel, letting it taper out to the front as seen in this photo.

Follow the guide lines and remove the excess material from the front corner of the foot. Caution: don't try to make the feet too thin! Some woods are brittle and have thin grains. Also cut the feet sloping out so while the feet look smaller, they still keep a good stable base.

Continue to carve out the tapered and sloping feet.

The foot should look roughly like this when you are done shaping it. Of course, you can always experiment with other options on your own.

If both feet are the same size you are really good! If not and you want to make them the same size, use the bottom of the feet and a piece of paper or cardboard to mark off the smaller foot and transfer that marking to the larger foot. Draw a straight line between the top and bottom points and you have a new guideline to follow. That will give you an equal foot size.

The penguin, being a three toed bird, needs three toes here to add character. Draw a center line down the foot and outline the toes like this. Remove the blackened in areas with a small cylinder burr with the 1/8" shank.

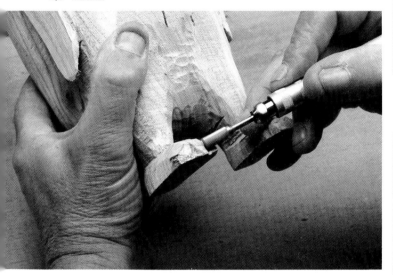

Cut the toes out, making V shaped cuts to give the toes a proper taper (cut from one direction and then the other to create the V).

Creating the V between the toes.

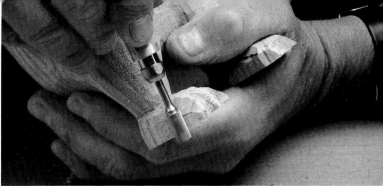

Take a little more off of the outside toe to get that third toe defined.

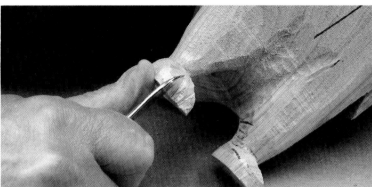

There is nothing wrong with using a good wood working knife to help sharply define those toes.

Remove a little material from the outer two toes to define the middle toe further. This provides a little extra character in a very simple manner.

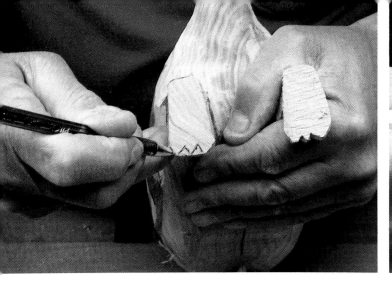

Transfer the toe pattern to the base of the other foot and repeat the toe cutting process.

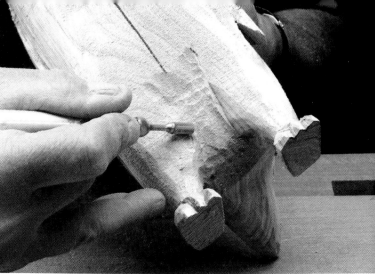

Use the 1/4" cylinder cutter to provide a little extra definition around the insides of the leg against the underbelly.

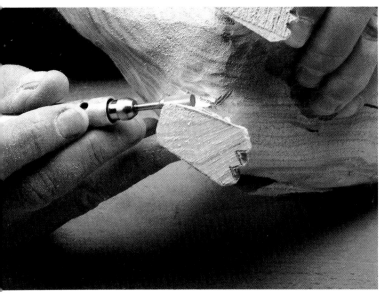

If you have any rough spots or marks between the legs this is a good time to clean them up.

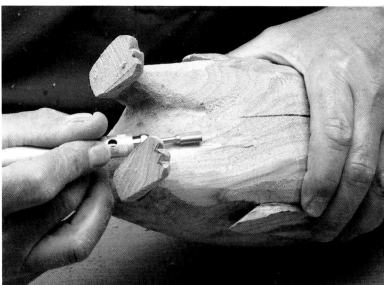

The easiest way to add that definition is to hold the cutter as shown and run it against the side of the leg.

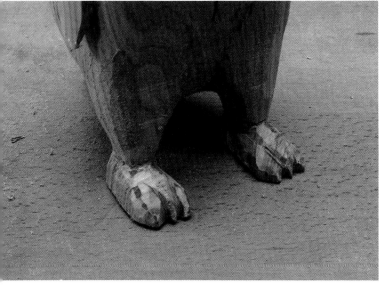

The finished feet before sanding.

To finish the inside of the beak you can use a round nose cutter as shown here or take a piece of sand paper and slide it back and forth as though shining a shoe with a rag.

Ready for sanding.

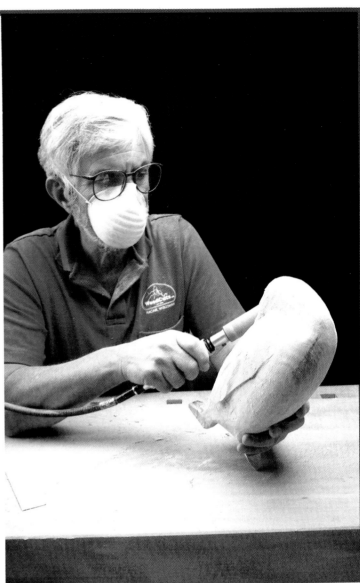

Remember while sanding to keep checking that both sides of your penguin remain symmetrical.

Take your sanding drum and your Swiss Gold sandpaper and let's go. Start with 120 grit sandpaper, graduating to 220 and then 320 after the first sanding. There is no particular place to start, just sand with the grain. Keep in mind this is going to be a clear finish piece, so the more care you take in sanding the better your piece will be. This is also the time to take care of all the nicks and dings you haven't removed earlier.

Make sure that your outlines are smooth. Here at the top of the head and neck is a good case in point.

A small piece of hand-held sandpaper works well in those small, hard-to-reach areas ... around the beak for instance.

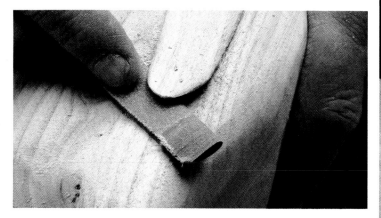

Folding a piece of sand paper over several times makes a quick and easy sanding stick for reaching under the wings.

I like to go around all the detail areas with this sanding stick as well to get rid of any scratch marks. It also works well for rounding the edges of the wings.

Now go over the entire piece, following the grain with your hand held sanding stick or a larger sheet of sand paper for broader surfaces. Be careful how you hold and prop your penguin during sanding. Remember, the feet aren't very thick anymore and we don't want to put a lot of extra pressure on them while sanding.

58

Nearly done. The major work is over, including the sanding.

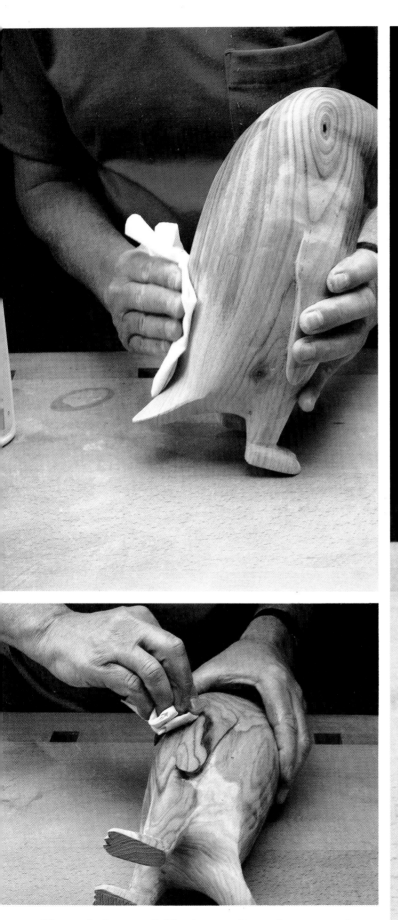

Now apply the tung oil. That is my preference but spray urethane, Danish oil or other finishes of good quality will work well also. Don't skimp here. You put a lot of work into this and you want it to look good, so use the 0000 steel wool between coats.

The finished penguin.

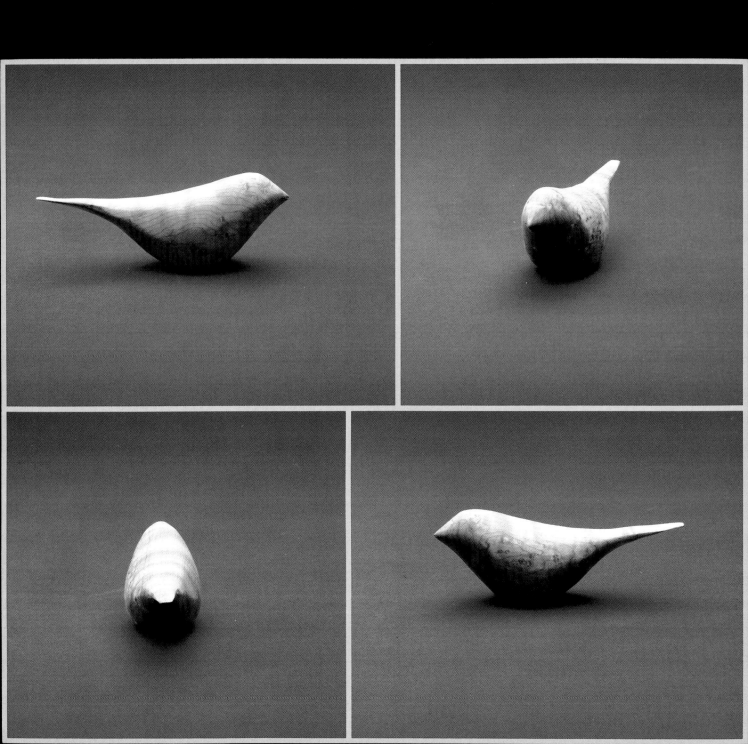